D1408462

COLLECTION EDITS BY
JUSTIN EISINGER & ALONZO SIMON

COLLECTION DESIGN BY
JEFF POWELL

WINTERWORLD CREATED BY
CHUCK DIXON AND JORGE ZAFFINO

ISBN: 978-1-63140-073-5

17 16 15 14 1 2 3 4

IDW®
www.IDWPUBLISHING.com
IDW founded by Ted Adams, Alex Garner, Kris Oprisko, and Robbie Robbins

WINTER WORLD

LA NIÑA

WRITTEN BY
CHUCK DIXON

ILLUSTRATED BY
BUTCH GUICE

COLORED BY
DIEGO RODRIGUEZ

LETTERED BY
ROBBIE ROBBINS AND TOM B. LONG

COVER BY
BUTCH GUICE & DIEGO RODRIGUEZ

SERIES EDITED BY
DAVID HEDGECOCK

1

IT HAS ALWAYS BEEN THIS WAY.

THE COLD. THE ICE.

THERE'S NO ONE ALIVE WHO REMEMBERS WHEN IT WAS DIFFERENT.

NO ONE REMEMBERS
NOT BEING HUNGRY.

NOT BEING COLD.

NOT BEING AFRAID.

EVERY DAY IS A FIGHT.
TIH-
TANG

ANY DAY COULD BE THE LAST.
TIH-
TANG
TANG
AND EVERY DAY, KNOWING IT CAN ALWAYS GET WORSE.
TIH-
TANG
TANG

BUT IN ALL THOSE DAYS OF COLD AND HUNGER AND FEAR—

–COULD I HAVE JUST *ONE* EASY DAY?
SHIT!
SHIT!

SHIT!
LANGUAGE, SCULLY.

AT LEAST IT'S *WARM*.
ENJOY IT WHILE YOU CAN BECAUSE THIS MOTOR IS *COOKED*, WYNN.

I *KNEW* WE SHOULD HAVE STOLEN THE HYBRID TRACTOR! BUT *SOMEONE* WANTED SOMETHING MORE ROOMY!

I THOUGHT WE *NEEDED* THE CARGO SPACE, SCULLY.
WHAT DO WE DO *NOW*?

WE WALK.

ESSENTIALS ONLY. STUFF THAT KEEPS US ALIVE.

NO BOOKS. YOU'RE GOING TO PULL, NOT READ.

ONE BOOK?
OKAY. ONE.
LES MISÉRABLES.
SURE. THE HEAVIEST ONE.

RAH-RAH!
WHERE'D THAT BADGER GET TO?

WELL, AT LEAST YOU HAVE SOMETHING TO BE HAPPY ABOUT.

MAYBE WE SHOULD GO *BACK*.
WHAT IF IT'S *LONGER* TO GO BACK THAN GO AHEAD?

WHAT IF IT'S *NOT*?
THEY'LL BE *PISSED* BACK AT EARTHFIRE. WE'D DO BETTER HEADING *WEST*. WE'RE HALFWAY THERE.

HALFWAY ACROSS THE *CARIBBEAN*? HOW DO YOU EVEN *KNOW* THAT?

LOOK, I'M NOT THE ONE WHO *CHANGED* HER MIND ABOUT FINDING YOUR PARENTS.
SHUT UP AND *PULL*.

YARK!
WHAT *IS* IT, BOY?

WHAT IS THAT, SCULLY?
NO IDEA. I'M JUST GLAD TO SEE SOMETHING OTHER THAN THE HORIZON.
THE VERY LEAST, WE CAN GET OUT OF THE WIND.
THERE MIGHT BE PEOPLE.
ALL THE WAY OUT HERE?
WE'RE OUT HERE.
A SHIP. A WAR SHIP.
THE CREW ABANDONED IT WHEN IT GOT ICE-STRUCK.
A LONG TIME AGO.

SEE? NO ONE. I THINK THEY'D HAVE TAKEN A SHOT AT US, WYNN.
UNLESS THEY WERE WAITING FOR US TO GET CLOSER.
RAH-RAH WOULD HAVE BARKED.
AND WHERE IS RAH-RAH NOW?
LOOK AT ALL THIS AMMUNITION. WE HAVE TO FIND OUR CALIBERS.
WE'VE BEEN THROUGH THE WHOLE BOAT. NOBODY HERE.
NOT THE WHOLE BOAT.
YOU WANT TO KEEP SCOUTING OR GO SHOPPING?
SHOPPING, STUPID.

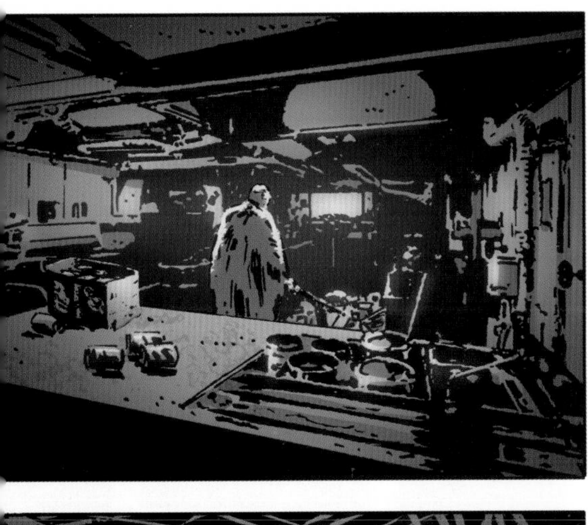

AUX. POWER MAIN
KACHINK!

OH, BABY...
...YOU'RE BEAUTIFUL.
COME ON... COME ON...
TUMP! TUMP.
YEAH.

I FOUND A *RIDE*. WE NEED TO LOOT, LOAD, AND *LEAVE*.
YOU GOT THE POWER *ON*.
YEAH, YEAH. NUCLEAR REACTOR. *MOVE* YOUR ASS.

BUT I WANT TO CHECK OUT THIS THING.
LEAVE IT!
BUT–
IT'S *JUNK*!
Loading...
Please Wait

I JUST WANTED TO PLAY WITH IT.
Loading
Please Wait

I THOUGHT WE WERE GONNA STAY HERE A WHILE.
Loading
Please Wait

NOW, WYNN!
ALL RIGHT! ALL RIGHT!

WE'RE LOADED AND OUT OF HERE. ALL YOU'RE GOING TO HAVE TO DO IS GUN IT HARD, WYNN.
I KNOW! I KNOW!
YOU'RE NOT GONNA MAKE THE GRADE UNLESS YOU–

GUN IT!
I GOT IT!
MUP!-GRRRRRRRRNNND!

HUNH!

OH!

OO!

DAMN IT!
STOP!

I WAS GOING TO COUNT TO THREE!
SO, WHY DIDN'T YOU?

WOLVES.
WE MUST BE GETTING CLOSE TO LAND.

TOLD YOU.
UH-HUH.
ANYTHING?

NOTHING. NO PLANE IN SIGHT.
DIDN'T MY GRANDFATHER TELL US THEY WENT NORTH?
NORTH. SOUTH. LIKE A COMPASS IS OF *ANY* USE.
MY HUNCH TELLS ME THEY WENT *WEST* TO THE NEAREST LAND MASS.

BETTER COME INSIDE.
JUST A COUPLE MINUTES...
ALL RIGHT THEN–

–I *WARNED* YOU.

MMM MM MHMMM MMM MMM—
NO! NO!

NO WOMAN NO CRY... NO WOMAN NO CRY...
NOT AGAIN, SCULLY!

MMM MM MHM... LIL' SISTER.
YOU HAVE A WOMAN, YOU KNOW. ME.
YOU? YOU'RE A GIRL!

NO WOMAN NO CRY...
MMF!
I MEAN, I DON'T THINK OF YOU AS A WOMAN... YOU'RE MORE LIKE...

A DAUGHTER?
HAHAHA HA
I WAS GONNA SAY A LITTLE SISTER!

BIENVENIDOS AL CANAL de PANAMA
WELL, I'M THE ONLY WOMAN IN YOUR LIFE.
JUST MY LUCK.

YOU'D MISS ME IF I WASN'T HERE.
WOULD I? ONE LESS MOUTH TO FIND FOOD FOR. ONE LESS ASS TO SAVE.

I CARRY MY WEIGHT AROUND HERE.
I'M A LONER, WYNN. I LIKE IT BETTER THAT WAY.

RIGHT. WHO WOULD YOU TALK TO IF I WASN'T HERE?
YOURSELF?
RAH-RAH?
RAH-RAH'S A GOOD LISTENER.

SCULLY...
I SEE IT. I SMELL IT.

YEEEEEEEK

YA YA YA!

SEE WHAT I'M *TALKING* ABOUT?
WHAT?

YOU *DO* NEED ME.
HOW WOULD YOU HAVE DONE *THIS* WITHOUT ME, SCULLY?

A *LADDER*, WYNN. JUST *POUR*, ALL RIGHT?

AND DO YOU *HAVE* A LADDER? NO, YOU...
...DON'T.

UM...

VRUUUUU-VRUUUUUUUU

GET DOWN THERE AND GET THE *MOTOR* GOING!
WHAT ARE *YOU* DOING?
SEEING HOW EASY THEY *DISCOURAGE*.

KKA-CHO OMMm!

I TOLD YOU TO *START* THE ENGINE, *NOT* DRIVE AWAY!
I'M CARRYING MY *WEIGHT*! I THOUGHT YOU'D BE *HAPPY*!

YOU'RE *STRIPPING* THE GEARS! WHERE ARE YOU *TAKING* US, WYNN?
AWAY FROM *THEM*, STUPID!

KKRASH

YOU'RE DRIVING US TOWARD A DEAD END! OFF!
UNNH!

YOU SAID YOU WERE GOING TO DISCOURAGE THEM!

WE'RE ON FIRE, SCULLY.

VRUUUUUU--- VRUUUUUU!

EAT TREAD, BASTARDS.
DID YOU HEAR ME? WE'RE ON FIRE.
AT LEAST IT'S WARM, RIGHT?

KERWHUMP
YAAAAAAAAK!

CRUSHED 'EM!
WYNN, BRACE YOURSELF.
WHY?

HERE COMES THAT DEAD END I WAS TALKING ABOUT.

BY WILL ROSADO & DIEGO RODRIGUEZ

2

I BLAME MYSELF.
I TAUGHT HER TO DRIVE.

WE'RE GONNA HIT- WE'RE GONNA HIT-WE'RE GONNA-
OH!
SCREEEEEEEEEE

RUMBLE

IT'S OKAY, RAH-RAH.
BE BRAVE. LIKE ME.

YIIIIIIII!
WHUMP

THERE'S THE OCEAN, SCULLY.
WHICH OCEAN?

EL OCÉANO PACÍFICO.
IT SAYS HERE THAT WE JUST WENT THROUGH SOMETHING CALLED THE PANAMA CANAL.

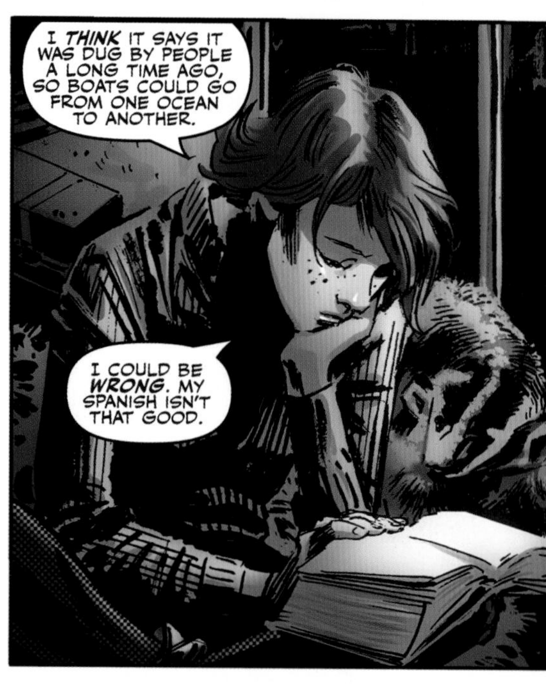
I THINK IT SAYS IT WAS DUG BY PEOPLE A LONG TIME AGO, SO BOATS COULD GO FROM ONE OCEAN TO ANOTHER.
I COULD BE WRONG. MY SPANISH ISN'T THAT GOOD.

WELL, THE MANUAL FOR THIS TRUCK IS IN ENGLISH. TRY READING THAT SO I KNOW WHAT KINDS OF FUEL I CAN TANK UP WITH.

"THE MAXXFORCE D9-X ENGINE IS A MULTI-CAPABLE PLANT SUITED TO ACCEPT DIESEL, GASOLINE, KEROSENE..."
OH YES, THIS IS FASCINATING.
KEEP READING, WYNN.

NO TENGO NINGUNA MADRE
NO TENGO NINGÚN PAPÁ
ESTOY SOLO EN EL MUNDO...

¿QUE?
DESPACIO, MIS AMIGOS.

HEY!
YOU SPEAK ANY ENGLISH?

GOT ANY CANNED PEACHES?

I HAVE NOTHING TO SPARE FOR TRADE, FORASTERO.
THAT'S ALL RIGHT. I ONLY WANT TO *TALK.*

YOU EVER SEE ANYTHING IN THE SKY? NOT A BIRD. SOMETHING WITH A MOTOR.

APPLE PIE FILLING...
SÍ. UN *AVIÓN*. I HAVE *SEEN* ONE.
WHEN?

ONLY A FEW *DAYS* AGO. IT SOARED OVERHEAD LIKE AN *ÁGUILA* THAT GROWLS.
HEAR THAT, RAH-RAH?

I SAW IT *THAT* WAY. *LÍNEA COSTERA*. I WATCHED UNTIL IT WAS FAR, *FAR* AWAY.
THERE IS *VILLAGE* THERE. IT IS CALLED *LA NIÑA*.

THANK YOU FOR THAT.
GRACIAS. I WISH YOU WELL.
GRAH-*SEE*-US...YOU *TOO*.

NO TENGO NINGUNA MADRE
NO TENGO NINGÚN PAPÁ
ESTOY SOLO EN EL MUNDO...
A PLANE? COULD IT BE...?
NO WAY TO KNOW, WYNN.

"BUT AT LEAST WE KNOW WHICH WAY WE'RE GOING."
"EVEN IF WE DON'T KNOW WHAT WE'LL FIND THERE."

IH?

MAN EATERS. DOG EATERS.

SKITTERS WANT TO *TALK*. TOO *MANY* MAN EATERS TO TALK.
SKITTERS MAKE *LESS* MAN EATERS.

YIYIYIYI!

CAN YOU TALK? YOU UNDERSTAND ME?
SÍ.

ESS-PAN-*YOL*? SKITTERS IS LOOKING FOR AN HOMBRE AND A NINA--A MAN AND GIRL.
SÍ?
AND A BADGER... *EL TEJÓN.*
UN HOMBRE Y UNA MUCHACHA EN UN TRINEO GRANDE. ELLOS FUERON AL MAR.
¿ESTO LO HACE FELIZ?

SÍ. THAT MAKES SKITTERS HAPPY.

WE FOLLOW THE COAST. MAPS ARE IRRELEVANT AND COMPASSES DON'T WORK.
ALL I CAN DO IS KEEP THE OCEAN TO MY RIGHT.
THE MAN SAID 'LAH NEEN-YAH?'

THAT'S WHAT HE *SAID*, WYNN. IT'S A VILLAGE WITH PEOPLE. WHAT'S IT *MEAN*?
LA...NEEEEN... YAAAAAAH....

La Niña
LOOKS LIKE IT MEANS "LITTLE GIRL."
SILLY NAME FOR A PLACE.

WHY WOULD ANYONE NAME A VILLAGE "LITTLE GIRL"?
MAYBE THE PLACE IS *RUN* BY LITTLE GIRLS.
OR MAYBE THEY CALLED IT THAT TO *FOOL* PEOPLE INTO THINKING IT'S SAFE.

EITHER WAY, I DON'T LIKE THE NAME MUCH.

THE GROUND RISES FROM THE COASTAL PLAIN A WEEK OR SO LATER.
I'M GONNA TAKE A PEEK IN THESE BUILDINGS.
COME ON, RAH-RAH.
LOOK FOR FOOD! NOT BOOKS!
OH... AND BE CAREFUL!

ALL HE THINKS OF IS HIS STOMACH.
BOOKS ARE GOOD TOO. STILL, I WOULDN'T MIND FINDING SOME CHOCOLATE.

OR SUGAR.

IGK.
TASTES LIKE MEDICINE.

MY TUG VEELS NUBB.
SNIF SNIF

WHAT THE HELL ARE YOU TWO *DOING*?
HOW ABOUT A *HAND* HERE?
HEE HEE HEE
YIP YIP

HUNH?

HA HA HA HA
YARK! YARK!

DO YOU THINK MY PARENTS ARE *AT* LAS NEEN-YUH? I THINK SO. I BET IT'S BEAUTIFUL AND SAFE AND *WARM*. THAT'S WHERE THEY'D *BE*, RIGHT, SCULLY? SOMEPLACE LIKE *THAT*. RIGHT? *RIGHT*?

SNARRRZZZZ

AND WHAT ARE THE RULES?

WE SHAKE THE CAN. IF IT CLUNKS IT'S NO GOOD. AND–
IF IT'S SWOLLEN IT'S NO GOOD. IF IT STINKS IT'S NO GOOD.
AND WHAT ELSE?

ASPARAGUS IS ONLY FOR TRADES.
SEE ANY CATFOOD? RAH-RAH LOVES THAT.

DON'T WORRY ABOUT MY BADGER–

–HE DOES FINE ON HIS OWN.

ONE OF MY BOOKS SAID PEOPLE RODE ON THESE THINGS.
AND THEY RUN ON SOMETHING. WE'LL FOLLOW THE TRACKS AND LOOK FOR FUEL.

WE LOSE SIGHT OF THE COASTLINE. THE MAPS SAY WE'RE STILL GOING SOUTH.

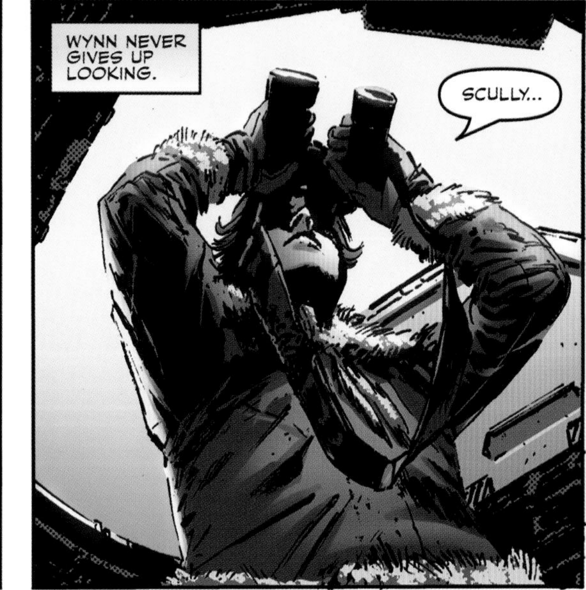
WYNN NEVER GIVES UP LOOKING.
SCULLY...

SCULLY!

SEA BIRDS AND...SMELL THAT?
SNIF SNIF
SMELL WHAT? WHAT IS IT?

SMELLS LIKE...
WHAT?
I DON'T KNOW!

DAMN IT, WYNN!

IT'S LIKE SPICE...AND SALT...
YIIIP

AND...

FEEL THAT, RAH-RAH?
RISING UP TO MEET US. WARM AIR.

UH?

TONIGHT.
WE WAIT FOR DARK.

GREEN PLANTS.

EVEN THE DIRT SMELLS GOOD. DID YOU SEE THE WATER?

I SAW IT, WYNN. LET'S BE QUIET, ALL RIGHT?

FOOD GROWING IN THE GROUND. WHAT DO YOU THINK THIS IS, SCUL?

WHY ASK ME? THERE'S NO LABEL, IS THERE? NOW PLEASE BE QUIET, WYNN.

SHIT.

KLAK-A-KLAK

BACK TO THE TRUCK!
RUN!
CHOOM!

SON OF A-
CHOOM!

-BITCH!

HUNH!

BLAM!
BLAM!
WHAT IS–

KLIK- KLIK- KLIK- KLIK
BASTARDS!

WHAT DO WE DO WITH THEM?
SCAVENGERS. WASTERS.
WE DO NOT NEED TWO MORE HUNGRY BELLIES.

THE MAN IS OF NO USE TO US. WE MIGHT USE THE GIRL.
I WILL TALK WITH THEM.

SCULLY, TELL ME YOU HAVE A PLAN. I WANT TO HEAR IT. I BET IT'S GOOD.

SORRY.
I'M SO SORRY, WYNN.

BY GERARDO ZAFFINO & DIEGO RODRIGUEZ

3

STICK OR MOVE.
THE ONLY CHOICES LIFE OFFERS YOU.
HIDE IN A WARM HOLE UNTIL YOU STARVE.
UNTIL SOMEONE TAKES *SOMETHING* AWAY FROM YOU.
OR GO ON THE ROAD AND TAKE YOUR CHANCES.

IT'S BEST TO STAY ON THE MOVE.
KAPOWW
MIERDA!
EVEN THOUGH YOU MEET *EVERY* BREED OF BASTARD.

BLAM

I *MIGHT* STICK SOMEPLACE SOMEDAY. WHO KNOWS?

I RIDE FROM PLACE TO PLACE LOOKING FOR SOMETHING BETTER.
I NEVER FIND IT.

AY... CABRÓN...
CHUNNNK!

I HAVE HIM!

KRAK!
UNNH!

YAAAAH

NO...

PUTA MADRE!
TAKE YOUR CHANCES. STICK OR MOVE.

LOOKS LIKE WYNN AND I ARE STICKING.
WE ARE *NOT* A CRUEL PEOPLE. IT IS ONLY THAT RESOURCES ARE *LIMITED*.

YOU UNDERSTAND. WE MUST *PROTECT* WHAT WE HAVE.
SO, LET US *GO*. YOU'LL NEVER SEE US AGAIN.

AND YOU WOULD *REMAIN* SILENT? YOU WOULD NOT TELL *OTHERS* OF LA NIÑA?
THEN JUST LET *ME* GO.

KEEP THE GIRL. AS A HOSTAGE.

LET ME GET BACK TO MY TRUCK AND I'M GONE.
A *TRUCK*?
YOU HAVE A TRUCK?

THIS TRUCK. IT CONSUMES FUEL?
YEAH. IT'S A BIG *THIRSTY* MOTHER, TOO.
WHAT KIND OF FUEL?

WHATEVER YOU GOT. GASOLINE. KEROSENE. DIESEL. ALCOHOL.

YOU CAN OPERATE AND *MAINTAIN* THIS ENGINE?
I GOT *THIS* FAR, DIDN'T I?
RELEASE HIM, BRAM.

AND YOU. WHAT ARE *YOU* TO THIS MAN?
SCULLY AND ME? WE'RE FRIENDS.

YOU ARE NOT... *MORE* THAN THAT TO HIM?
HUH?

HUFF!

SHE IS WELCOME HERE, TOO.

OH!

OOH!

UH!

CAMIÓN.

CAMIÓN GRANDE.

IT IS A GIANT! A BEAUTIFUL BEHEMOTH!
YEAH. IT'S ROOMY.

I HAVE NEVER SEEN AN OPERATING COMBUSTION ENGINE.
KEEPING IT RUNNING IS A LOST ART, NO?
MORE LIKE A KNACK.

I WILL SHOW YOU THE ROAD DOWN TO LA NIÑA.
YEAH. I GUESS.

INCREDIBLE.

THAT'S NOT NECESSARY, FRIEND. I'M NOT LEAVING WYNN BEHIND.
YOU WERE READY TO ABANDON HER BEFORE.
THINGS CHANGE, ALRIGHT?

YOU'RE UNDER PROBATION. JUST DRIVE.
YEAH, YEAH.

SEE-OH-TOO!
SEE-OH-TOO!
SEE-OH-TOO!
SEE-OH-TOO!
SEE-OH-TOO! SEE-OH-TOO!

IS THAT SOME KIND OF LOCAL GREETING?
THEY ARE VERY HAPPY. YOU BRING US HOPE.
I BRING YOU A TRUCK, OSHIDA.

...MUY BELLA...

UNA BELLEZA...

THE SOIL IS WARM, WYNN. WE CAN GROW ROOT VEGETABLES HERE AND DRY THEM. THEY KEEP FOR YEARS.
I'VE ONLY SEEN THIS IN PICTURES IN BOOKS.

SO GREEN.
HOW'S THIS POSSIBLE?

"IT IS CALLED EL NIÑO. SOME YEARS, THE TEMPERATURE OF THE SEA RISES. THE WARM WATERS BRING OUR SETTLEMENT BACK TO LIFE.
"WE GROW WHILE WE CAN AND PREPARE FOR THE TIMES WHEN THE COLD RETURNS.

"WE PULL FISH FROM THE SEA. WE COLLECT SALT FROM THE WATER. ALL WHILE EL NIÑO VISITS."

SO, YOU CALL THIS PLACE LA NIÑA. A GIRL TO ATTRACT A BOY.
EXACTLY. IT IS THE NATURAL ORDER.

I'VE NEVER SMELLED ANYTHING LIKE THIS PLACE BEFORE.
THAT IS THE SCENT OF THE PAST, WHEN THE WORLD WAS WARM AND GREEN.

HOW CAN I HELP HERE? I REALLY WANT TO DO SOMETHING.
EVERYONE HAS A ROLE TO PLAY HERE. EVEN YOU, WYNN.

WE HAVE GATHERED FUEL IN ANTICIPATION OF THE ARRIVAL OF SOMEONE LIKE YOU.
WE'VE RANGED AS FAR AS WE DARE FROM LA NIÑA TO SCAVENGE THIS MUCH.
SHIT. I'VE NEVER SEEN A STOCKPILE LIKE THIS.

I COULD RUN THE TRUCK FOREVER ON THIS MUCH, OSHIDA.
AS LONG AS SHE HOLDS UP ANYWAY.
THUNK

THEN YOU HAVE A HOME HERE, SCULLY.

SO WHERE IS IT THAT YOU WANT TO *GO* IN THE TRUCK?
GO?
WE DO NOT WISH TO GO *ANYWHERE*.

THEN WHY IS EVERYONE SO EXCITED ABOUT MY TRUCK?
BECAUSE IT BURNS THE FOSSIL FUELS THAT BRING THE *GREENHOUSE* TO LIFE.

GREENHOUSE?
THE WORLD IS COLD BECAUSE THE SKIES ARE DEPLETED OF CARBON DIOXIDE.
THERE WERE ONCE *MILLIONS* OF TRUCKS AND CARS.

THEY KEPT THE EARTH *WARM*. WE CAN *RETURN* THE WORLD TO THOSE DAYS.
THE BOOK IS VERY *CLEAR* ON THIS.

TO RESTORE THE BALANCE, WE MUST FILL THE AIR WITH POLLUTION. IT IS THE *ORDER* OF THINGS AS DETAILED IN THE WORDS OF GORE.
AL GORE
LA TIERRA EN JUEGO
UN PROPOSITO COMU
HUH.

I DON'T READ SPANISH.
IT IS SIMPLE ENOUGH. ELEGANT EVEN.
MAN CONTROLS THE FATE OF THIS PLANET.

THE WORLD WARMS AND COOLS BECAUSE OF OUR ACTIONS AND WE HAVE BEEN FOUND WANTING. WE HAVE NOT DONE OUR PART AND SO WE ARE CURSED WITH ICE.

WE WILL RECREATE THE GREENHOUSE AND MAKE THE WORLD ANEW.
YEAH?
STARTING WITH YOUR AMAZING MACHINE.

THE WARM, HEALING VAPORS WILL RISE AND THE CLOUDS WILL PART AND THE SUN WILL ONCE MORE–

HRAAK! KAFF! KAFF!

UM, TOO MUCH OF A GOOD THING, MAYBE?
KAKK KAFF!

THEY'RE *CRAZY.*
EVERY GODDAMN *ONE* OF THEM.

WHO *ISN'T* CRAZY, SCULLY?
WHO DOES IT HURT?
THEY THINK RUNNING OUR TRUCK IS GOING TO RE-HEAT THE PLANET.

IT HURTS *US* IF IT DOESN'T WORK.
DISAPPOINTMENT CAN BE AN UGLY THING, WYNN.

THEY *WATCH* US ALL THE TIME. WE NEED TO START THINKING ABOUT HOW WE'RE GONNA GET OUT OF HERE.
NOW WHO'S CRAZY? *I'M* NOT LEAVING LA NIÑA.

I LIKE IT HERE.

OH SHIT.

LOOK, IT'S ALL HOT FOOD AND GIGGLES RIGHT NOW. BUT THAT WON'T LAST. IT NEVER *DOES*.
THEN I'LL STAY AS *LONG* AS IT LASTS.

WHAT ABOUT FINDING YOUR *PARENTS?* ISN'T THAT *WHY* WE'RE HERE?
I *STILL* WANT TO FIND THEM. I'M JUST TIRED OF MOVING *ALL* THE TIME.
MOVE OR *DIE*, WYNN.

I DON'T WANT TO THINK ABOUT WHAT *MIGHT* HAPPEN, SCULLY. I WANT TO *NOT* THINK ABOUT TOMORROW FOR A WHILE.
I JUST WANT TO BE HAPPY *NOW*.

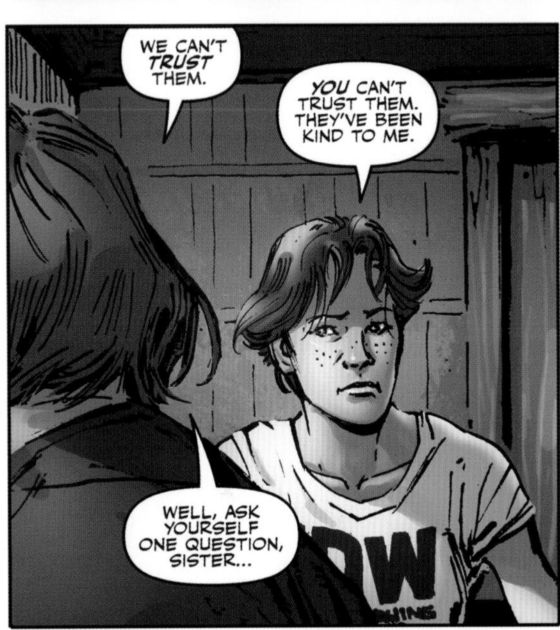
WE CAN'T *TRUST* THEM.
YOU CAN'T TRUST THEM. THEY'VE BEEN KIND TO ME.
WELL, ASK YOURSELF ONE QUESTION, SISTER...

...WHERE'S RAH-RAH?
WHY'S *HE* STILL HIDING FROM THEM?

STUPID KID...

UH?
IT IS GETTING COLDER AT NIGHT.
FEELS WARM TO *ME*. IT'S WONDERFUL.

STILL, IT IS COLD. THE WARM CURRENT IS LEAVING US. THE OLDER PEOPLE SAY SO.
IT WILL BE TIME FOR A NEW *GATHERING* SOON.
WHAT'S THAT?

WE PRAY AND SING AND WELCOME EL NIÑO BACK TO OUR SHORE.
YOU'LL BE THERE FOR THIS ONE.
YOU'RE SO LUCKY, STEPHAN. YOU HAVE A *FAMILY* HERE.

IT'S LONELY OUT THERE. THERE ARE ONLY PEOPLE WHO WANT TO *TAKE* FROM YOU.
YOU ARE *WELCOME* HERE. YOU WILL BECOME *ONE* OF US. YOU WILL BE *LOVED* BY ALL.

EVEN YOU?

NO...NO... I CANNOT...

THAT'S THE STUFF...

WHAT'S IN THE MASH, BRAM?
STEMS. LEAVES. WHATEVER WE TEAR UP WHEN THE CROPS ARE DEPLETED. YOUR TRUCK CAN RUN ON THIS, RIGHT?
HELL, *I* CAN RUN ON IT.

HARSH.
BUT *DAMN* GOOD.

YOU CAN *DRINK* IT?
CUTS THE *CHILL*. MAKES THE *LADIES* PRETTIER. HAVE A TASTE.

GET SOME *FIRE* IN YOUR BELLY, SON.

WYNN...

STEPHAN?
HEY...

BACK OFF!
HOLD ON... WE'RE ALL HERE.

ALL?
YOUR NEW FAMILY.
IT'S TIME FOR THE GATHERING, WYNN.

YOU WANT ME THERE?
WE NEED YOU THERE. YOU ARE TO BE THIS YEAR'S LA NIÑA.

ESTA ES LA NOCHE... ESTA ES LA NOCHE DE LA NIÑA.

THE *TIME* HAS COME. THE *SEA* GROWS COLD. THE *ICE* RETURNS.
EL NIÑO ABANDONS US TO DAYS AND NIGHTS OF KILLING COLD–

–UNLESS *LA NIÑA* CAN WOO HIM BACK TO OUR SHORE.

WILL *YOU* OFFER YOUR CHARMS TO BRING YOUR FAMILY WARM DAYS?
I WILL.
HEE.

THEN *YOU* WILL WEAR THE BELL.
AND TAKE THE BLESSINGS OF US *ALL* WITH YOU.

BY GERARDO ZAFFINO & DIEGO RODRIGUEZ

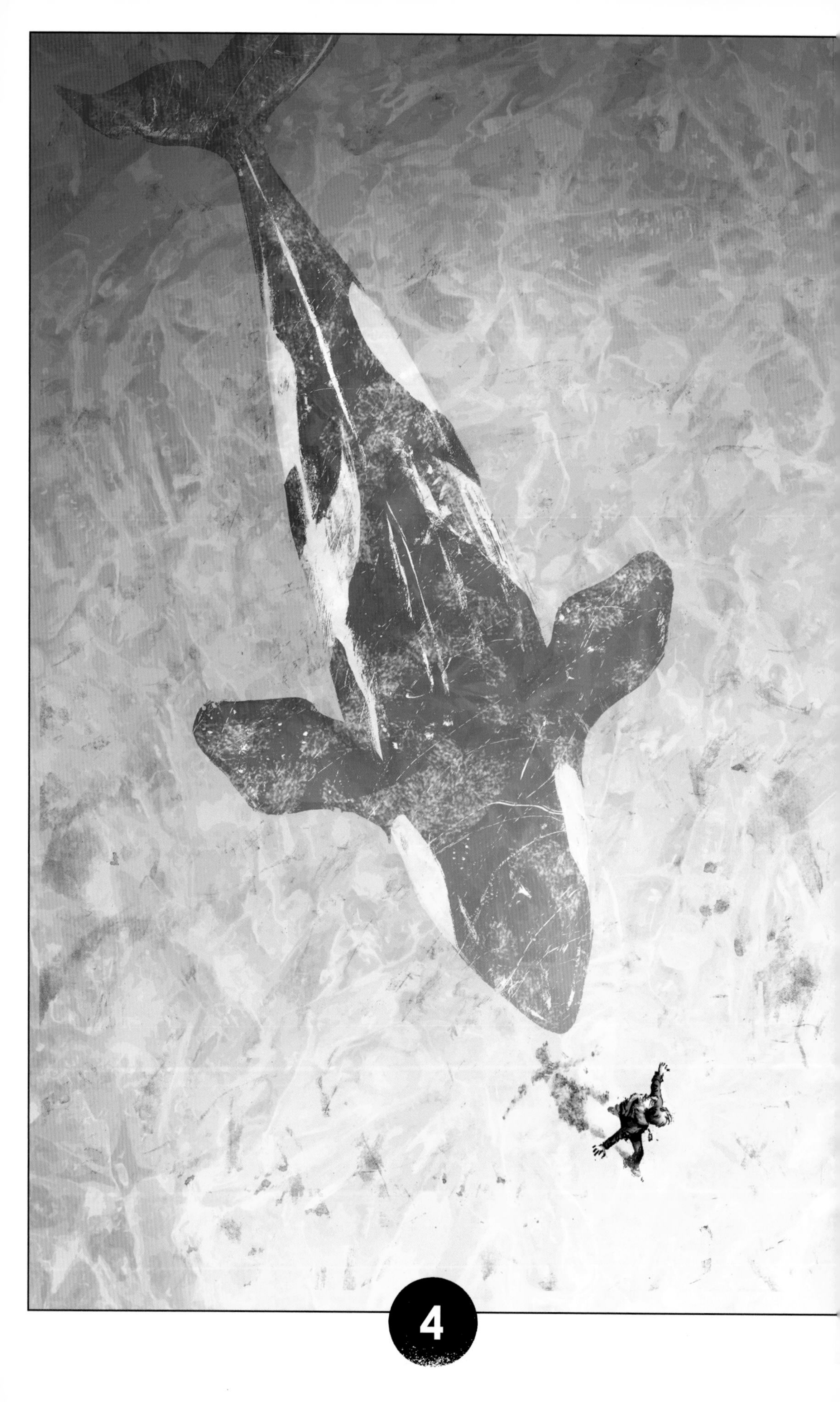
4

BRAM?
YOU *IN* THERE, BRAM?

OSHIDA WANTS THE *WASTER* BROUGHT DOWN TO SEE THE CEREMONY.

BRAM?

SHOW YOURSELF, WASTER.

RIGHT *HERE*, ASSHOLE.
WHUMP
UNNH!
WHERE'S THE *GIRL*?
TOO LATE...

WHERE'S *WYNN?* TALK WHILE YOU HAVE A *HEAD*.

SHE IS DOWN AT THE JETTY FOR THE *CEREMONY*.
SHE IS *NOT* LEAVING. NEITHER ARE *YOU*.

THE PLACE IS QUIET.
LIGHTS OUT AND LANES EMPTY.

JUST TWO GUYS TO WATCH MY RIDE.

I COULD TAKE THEM AND DRIVE AWAY.
DAMN YOU, WYNN.

DAMN *ME*.

WHAT ARE THESE CRAZIES UP TO?

SHIT.

WYNN?

TIH-TANG-TANG
I'M NOT SURE I *GET* THIS.
HOW *FAR* AM I SUPPOSED TO WALK?

I MEAN, THIS IS AN *HONOR* AND ALL.
BUT I'M NOT SURE WHAT I'M SUPPOSED TO BE *DOING*.

YOU SAID IT *YOURSELF*, WYNN.
EL NIÑO NEEDS LA NIÑA. *YOU* WILL BRING HIM TO US. YOU WILL BRING *SPRING* AGAIN.

THAT'S *GREAT,* MARTINE.
ONLY THE ICE IS GETTING KIND OF *THIN* HERE.
TANK TANG

IT WILL GROW *THICKER* FARTHER OUT.

OKAY THEN.
TIH- TANG

JUST A LITTLE WALK ON THE ICE.
TIH- TONK

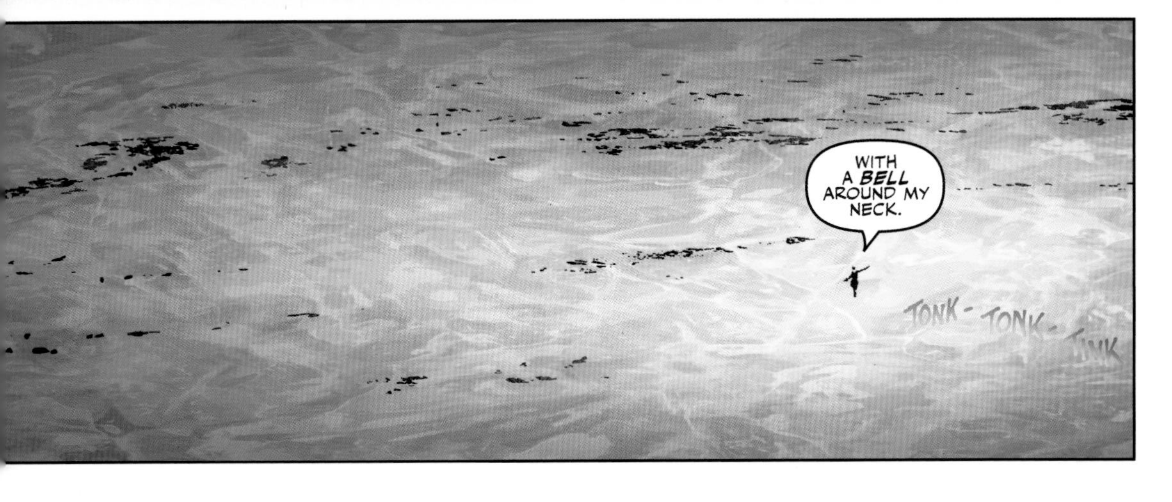
WITH A *BELL* AROUND MY NECK.
TONK- TONK- TINK

ALL-
-ALONE.

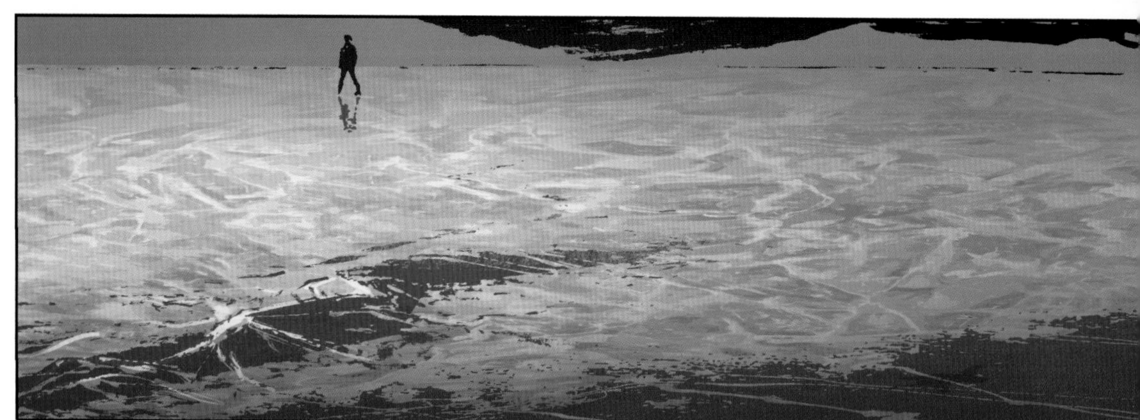

TIH-TANG-TANG-TANG-TANG

TANG-TANG-TANG-TANG

TANG-TANG TANG-TANG-TANG

EL NIÑO, MY ASS.

BLONG--- BLONGGG---
SHIT!

THAT'S IT, SUCKER.
NICE *BIG* BELL FOR YOU.

NO!
BASTARD MUST HEAR ME RUNNING.

OR SMELL ME.

PANT... SHIT!... PANT...
TING
TING
TING

STINKING BELL!

THEY PICK YOU TOO? YOU LAST YEAR'S VIRGIN?

KRRRRKKKK
KRRRRKKK
MAN...
TANG
UH!

TING TING
COME ON!
LET GO, BITCH!

ALL RIGHT, NIÑO.
LET'S HAVE A LOOK AT YOU.

AND PLEASE DON'T HAVE LEGS.

OH.
TING-TANG!

HUNH!
TANG-TANG!

HA!
CAN'T **REACH** ME, SUCKER!

GOOD LUCK WITH YOUR **NEXT** NIÑA!

YEAH, BONES...
...YOU WON *TOO*, HUH?

FREEZE, STARVE, OR BE EATEN. LIKE TOM AND BECKY LOST IN THE CAVE.
THERE'S *GOT* TO BE ANOTHER PATH.
"THERE'S *GOT* TO BE A WAY OUT OF HERE."

I DO NOT *HEAR* THE BELL.
SHE MADE IT *PAST* THE BUOY.

EL NIÑO HAS ACCEPTED HIS NEW BRIDE.
WARMING SEAS WILL BE OURS IF HE IS PLEASED.

HE WILL BE PLEASED. THE OMENS ARE STRONG. A NEW SPRING AND THE WASTER'S TRUCK WILL RESTORE THE GREENHOUSE.
ALL UNDER YOUR WISE GUIDANCE, OSHIDA. BUT WHAT ABOUT THE WASTER?

"SCULLY IS ONLY OF USE TO US UNTIL WE HAVE LEARNED THE SECRETS OF THE FOSSIL FUEL ENGINE.
"BUT NOW, WE CELEBRATE!"

YOU'RE A STUBBORN FISH, HUH?
WELL, I'M NOBODY'S BAIT!
YOU HEAR THAT, FISH?

MISSED ME, PUSSY!
YOU GONNA TRY AGAIN, PUSSY?
NO...
SCULLY...
WHERE ARE YOU, YOU BASTARD...?

KA-BLAM!
KA-BLAM!
KA-BLAM!

WYNN!
THIS WAY!
JEEZE, SCULLY! YOU TOOK YOUR SWEET TIME!
HAD TO GET AWAY FROM MY KEEPERS.

TIH-TANG-TANG-TA NG-TANG-TANG-TANG
HEY, WE'RE NOT OUT OF THIS YET, GIRL.
I THOUGHT... I WAS ALONE... I THOUGHT...
YOU THOUGHT I'D LEAVE YOU BEHIND?

WHO'S GONNA READ TO ME?

MICKEY SPILLANE ALL DAY LONG. PROMISE.

DID EL NIÑO HAVE A *SISTER?* YOU KNOW, FOR *ME?*
SHUT UP, SCULLY!

WHAT ARE WE GOING TO DO?
WELL, THESE JACKASSES WILL BE BUSY HAVING A *PARTY*. SO WE JUST TAKE THE TRUCK AND GET THE HELL *OUT* OF HERE.

"WE'LL BE *GONE* BEFORE THEY KNOW IT."
MY ENGINE... MY BEAUTIFUL, FOSSIL FUEL ENGINE...

WHERE *IS* IT?

WHERE *IS* IT?

NONE OF THESE MORONS KNEW HOW TO *DRIVE*, RIGHT?
THAT'S WHAT THEY *TOLD* ME.
SOMEONE WAS *LYING*. THEY LIED TO YOU AND THEY LIED TO *OSHIDA*.

WHAT NOW?
WHAT DO YOU THINK? SOMEONE STOLE MY TRUCK. SOME DIRTY SON OF A BITCH STOLE MY GODDAMN TRUCK.

MMM... WOMAN NO CRY...
"WE'RE GOING TO FIND THEM AND MAKE THEM SORRY."

MMM... WOMAN NO CRY...

NO WOMAN NO CRY... NO WOMAN NO CRY...

MMM... WOMAN NO CRY...

THEY'LL TAKE THAT COAST ROAD. FOLLOW THE RAIL TRACKS.
WE'RE GOING TO CHASE THEM ON FOOT? WE'LL NEED FOOD. SUPPLIES.

AND WE KNOW WHERE TO FIND THEM.
WE'LL ALSO NEED A DISTRACTION.

RAH-RAH!
WHERE'S HE BEEN?

YOU HAVE BETRAYED US. YOU HAVE LET THE ANSWER TO OUR PRAYERS ROLL AWAY.

YOU ARE A TRAITOR, BRAM!
THE WASTER TRICKED ME... POISONED ME.
YOU SAID HE DRANK THIS 'POISON' HIMSELF.

¿QUE?
THE BARN IS ON FIRE!

"THEY WANTED IT HOT. THEY GOT IT HOT."
ANYWAY THEY WON'T BE FOLLOWING US. LET'S GET OUR TRUCK BACK.
AND MY BOOKS.
SURE.
AND MY HAT. THAT WAS A GREAT HAT.
MORE HIKE, LESS TALK, LA NIÑA.
YARK!
THE END OF WINTERWORLD: LA NIÑA

BY GERARDO ZAFFINO & DIEGO RODRIGUEZ